Breeding Zebra Finches
KW-056

Contents

Acknowledgements: I'd like to acknowledge the large amount of help I received while writing this book. Plenty of good solid help came from wholesaler A.A. Buzz Pare, breeder Garrie Landry, birdkeeper Daniel Kaye, veterinarian Robert S. Clark, and ever-patient typist Edith F. Roberts.

Photographers and artists: D.J. Baron, G. Ebben, Michael Gilroy, Keith Hindwood, Paul Kvast, Harry V. Lacey, R. and V. Moat, Tierfreunde, A. van der Nieuwenhuizen, Mervin F. Roberts, Heinz Schrempp, W. Starika, Vogelpark Walsrode, R.A. Vowles, Dr. M. Vriends, J. Wessels.

Distributed in the UNITED STATES by T.F.H. Publications, Inc., One T.F.H. Plaza, Neptune City, NJ 07753; in CANADA to the Pet Trade by H & L Pet Supplies Inc., 27 Kingston Crescent, Kitchener, Ontario N2B 2T6; Rolf C. Hagen Ltd., 3225 Sartelon Street, Montreal 382 Quebec; in CANADA to the Book Trade by Macmillan of Canada (A Division of Canada Publishing Corporation), 164 Commander Boulevard, Agincourt, Ontario M1S 3C7; in ENGLAND by T.F.H. Publications Limited, Cliveden House/Priors Way/Bray, Maidenhead, Berkshire SL6 2HP, England; in AUSTRALIA AND THE SOUTH PACIFIC by T.F.H. (Australia) Pty. Ltd., Box 149, Brookvale 2100 N.S.W., Australia; in NEW ZEALAND by Ross Haines & Son, Ltd., 18 Monmouth Street, Grey Lynn, Auckland 2, New Zealand; in SINGAPORE AND MALAYSIA by MPH Distributors (S) Pte., Ltd., 601 Sims Drive, #03/07/21, Singapore 1438; in the PHILIPPINES by Bio-Research, 5 Lippay Street, San Lorenzo Village, Makati Rizal; in SOUTH AFRICA by Multipet Pty. Ltd., 30 Turners Avenue, Durban 4001. Published by T.F.H. Publications, Inc. Manufactured in the United States of America by T.F.H. Publications, Inc.

BREEDING ZEBRA FINCHES

MERVIN F. ROBERTS

Above: *A fawn male zebra finch. Note the seamless band on its right leg.*
Right: *A group of mixed zebras husking seeds right back into their food tray.*

Introducing Zebra Finches

Many advanced and experienced aviculturists who long ago mastered the breeding of rare, delicate and difficult species have never given up on their zebras—this much in the same vein as those tropical fish hobbyists who have bred discus fish and cardinal tetras but never gave up their guppies. The simple truth is that many people enjoy breeding zebra finches without regard to how easy it is.

Breeding zebras is so easy it almost doesn't justify a book. They do it by themselves. The basics could be printed on the side panel of a pound box of bird seed. Yet this book and other books about zebra finches have been written, edited, illustrated, printed, published, sold and read by the thousands all over the world. The reason is that although it is easy to propagate a few birds by the application of beginners' luck, it is another matter to do it well.

This, then, is a book about ways to do it well. Read it through from cover to cover. Initially omit the genetics if this gets a little sticky the first time. Your specific questions will certainly find ready answers as time and your reading go on.

In this book the main thrust is toward helping you succeed in

breeding your birds. A companion book entitled *Zebra Finches* puts more emphasis on varieties, general care and history. The two books do overlap, but every effort has been made to separate the information for the bird keeper from the information for the breeder.

Several of the photographs which appear in this book were taken in an aviary created especially for close observation of breeding birds. The enclosed area is eight feet by twelve feet and the ceiling slopes down from six feet to three feet. The floor is a continuous piece of kitchen-type textured material and two walls and the ceiling are sheetrock painted with white latex. The other two walls are 1/2-inch square galvanized wire mesh, and the outside flight is reached through the window which may be closed during inclement weather. In the course of two winters in Connecticut it was never fully closed. The outside flight is double-screened. Its outside screen is a copper mesh mosquito netting, and on the inside of the 2" x 4" frame is again the 1/2-inch square galvanized mesh. The wooden floor of the flight is sloped to drain (1/4-inch per foot) and it is covered with beach sand. The perches are mostly potted shrubs.

NAMES AND PLACES

Suffice it to say here that we are considering the bird which English-speaking people call the zebra or zebra finch. In the past it has been sometimes called the chestnut-eared finch. The French commonly call it the *diamant mandarin* and the German, Danish and Swedish fanciers call it *zebra fink.*

Scientifically there is some difference of opinion among the taxonomists. Don't get the idea that because a name is scientific, it is here to stay. Some recent authorities dogmatically tell us that this bird should be called *Taeniopygia guttata castanotis* or perhaps just plain *Taeniopygia guttata,* and others are equally dogmatic in their calling it *Poephila guttata.* In 1817, Vieillot called it *Fringilla guttata;* and 1837, Gould called it *Amadina castanotis.* Let's simply call it the zebra finch and no one in the English-speaking world will confuse it with another bird.

So much for names—now for places. This is easy. Zebra finches originate from all of Australia except for the rainforest. A subspecies (or perhaps it is a race) also appears on the Lesser Sunda Islands just north of that great island continent. For a really thorough treatment of the distribution and geographic variation of this bird you should

A crested fawn zebra finch. The zebra finch is among the easiest birds to breed; however, breeding good quality zebras requires much research and patience.

read Immelmann's *Australian Finches in Bush and Aviary*. All zebra finches outside Australia are from stocks which are bred in captivity. There are no wild birds being exported from that country.

Above: *The bright red bill of this zebra finch proves it to be a male.* **Right:** *Zebras can be kept with most other small finches such as these blue-capped waxbills.*

Behavior

ACTIVITY

Whether you have one bird or a hundred, there will be active periods and quiet periods. Of course, all zebra finches remain quiet during the dark hours, but during daylight hours a zebra is not constantly on the go. You may witness ten or fifteen minutes of bathing followed by an equal period of drying and preening. Later there might be a ten minute mealtime and a twenty minute snooze, then another meal or nest-making or a sunning and preening interlude and so on through the day. It is perfectly normal for a healthy zebra finch to snooze at midday.

Obviously a bird with its head tucked underneath its wing all day is sick and needs isolation, warmth, antibiotics and professional help. With only a

little luck, a little work and a patient application of your powers of observation and intelligence, you will probably be able to maintain your birds for years with no problem other than the need to clip their nails. And if you plant reeds and supply some rough stones, then even clipping might not be necessary.

Young birds will sit on the aviary or cage floor and wait to be fed. Adult birds will perch on twigs or dowels. An adult that sits on the floor is probably sick or about to die. At night, young and adults frequently roost in nests which they build especially for nighttime use. An adult male frequently guides the young

A pair of white zebra finches. The female is the heavier of the two birds.

A gray zebra finch. In the wild, the reproduction of zebra finches is dependent upon the rainy season in Australia.

birds to the nest of their birth or to a roosting nest nightly for several weeks.

Why do young babies leave their nest? I imagine that it is nature's way that the nest cavity will fill up as the young birds develop. Parents will naturally continue to add grass, the young will naturally defecate around the rim and after the first few days this material will not be removed; in the meantime the babies will naturally continue to grow. Within fifteen days, each baby will be about ten times the volume of the egg from which it hatched. All this naturally tends

to force the fledglings out of their nest. They cannot remain simply because there isn't enough room. This pressure to speed things up is, I would speculate, a function of the Australian midcontinent climate. The rains stimulate plant growth and the birds capitalize on the available short term food supply, but they must work fast because the rainy season will not continue very long, and the urge to reproduce is strong.

THE PECKING ORDER

Chickens are famous for their henhouse and barnyard pecking

Above: *Zebras are great birds for togetherness. Here one preens while the other rests.* **Opposite:** *The bird with the ruffled feathers on its head is not injured; this is just a poor grade crest. Note the claws on these birds—they are of normal length and need not be clipped.*

orders, and psychologists have climbed the ladder to academic acclaim by writing papers about these pecking orders. It goes on everywhere, all the time.

When the pecking order syndrome is applied to zebra finches, you will discover that a single pair does well together. Three or four pairs stimulate each other to breed more frequently, but given two pairs or an odd bird in a small group, you may experience trouble.

A simplistic explanation is that zebras cannot count to much over four or five. A cage or aviary with a half dozen birds will not have a pecked or picked-on bird on the bottom of the ladder because no other bird remembers which is which.

I'm reminded of the dreaded piranha of the Amazon River which, when kept in an aquarium, must be solitary since it will destroy or be destroyed. There has been for many years a display tank in the Shedd Aquarium in Chicago with three or four dozen of these fish. Even though now and then one might get nipped, there was no widespread mayhem. If,

however, the fish were separated into groups of perhaps three, the results would surely be fatally bloody. So, keep a pair or a half-dozen birds together, but avoid two pairs in the same cage or aviary.

COURTSHIP

Both the male and the female are prone to hop back and forth between branches of a tree or shrub. They indulge in beak wiping and tail twisting. The male zebra finch, in contrast to some other finches, does not carry a grass stem in his beak during courtship. The male dances, stands tall and puffs his body feathers; if the female permits, copulation takes place on a twig in the open. They may copulate several times. Sometimes the female will mount the male. There will be a good deal of preening of each bird by the other.

Once paired, zebra finches seem to settle down for life and although they can be separated and re-paired, the normal procedure would be a lifetime pairing—even when the birds are part of a flock or are in a large well-stocked aviary. This has been my experience; other fanciers report that male zebra finches are real Don Juans.

THE NEST

Shrubs and low trees are favored by birds in the wild. Aviary and cage birds do very well with covered nest baskets. In the wild or in captivity these birds will frequently choose thorny shrubs; rosebushes and berry bushes are common nest sites. A juniper tree in my aviary was always the site of at least two nests although baskets and nest boxes were also available. The zebra finch is adaptable and flexible. Sometimes they will nest in hollow trees or even holes in the ground! Most nests are built at heights under ten feet.

The exterior of the nest is coarse and is constructed of twigs and grass stems. It is lined with soft material—feathers, if available. Rabbit fur, wool, cotton rags, bits of string and plant down are employed if available. The nest is domed and the entrance is on the side. Roosting nests are sometimes also constructed, but these are not lined with soft materials. If the birds start a second family before the first is on its own, the roosting nest may then be used as a breeding nest.

The male selects the nesting material and delivers it to the

Opposite: *A breeding pair of zebra finches. Zebras are prone to mating for life.*

Above: *A wild female zebra finch in her nest, which is built of twigs and roots. Cage and aviary birds are more likely to settle for grass leaves and stems.* **Opposite:** *Six eggs in a half of a coconut. This is a popular nest site in the author's aviary.*

A male zebra finch. This is the original and still most popular color. The orange cheek patches and vivid colors indicate a male bird.

nest site. The female frequently does most of the construction work. A nest is usually completed from scratch in a week; completion never takes more than two weeks.

Zebras will sometimes stack their nests even if they are not crowded. This leads to loss of eggs and is usually discouraged by experienced birdkeepers. Discouraging a zebra finch from stacking nests is easier said than done.

When the nest is completed or nearly completed, the first egg will be laid. Rainy weather seems to stimulate these birds to breed, but under ideal conditions they will keep it up all year long.

An average nest will have five smooth white eggs, but three or ten are frequently laid. The adults will begin to incubate the eggs after the fifth or maybe after the fourth egg is laid. The eggs generally appear at the rate of one per day, but sometimes a day is skipped.

Each parent will spend an hour or two on the nest during daylight hours and one will get off before the other gets on. Sometimes a few minutes will

Zebra finches are hardy little birds which do well in captivity. A good diet and suitable surroundings are just about the only necessities these birds have.

Above: *This nest basket was not emptied after its first occupancy. That was a mistake. The remaining space is simply insufficient for another clutch.* **Opposite:** *A comparison of zebra finch eggs (group of four) with the eggs of a Gouldian finch. The eggs of these species are quite similar.*

elapse between the departure of one parent and the arrival of the other. (This is not universal among birds; some birds switch on the nest—obviously a northern sea-bird could not do otherwise, considering the predators and the cold.) Both parent zebras occupy the nest at night.

After 12 to 16 days of incubation the eggs hatch and both parents actively feed the young. One or two birds will sometimes hatch a day after the first come out of their shells. Sometimes as these babies leave the nest the male will continue to feed them while the female starts a new clutch of eggs in the same nest, in an old nest or in a nest they built previously for roosting. The adult birds seem to be flexible as they make these family arrangements. These birds are very social and although the pair bond is tight, precise protocols and procedures seem to be lacking.

Zebra finch eggs are white. When they are laid they have a creamy tint. When they are about to hatch they have a gray tint due to the color of the embryo. Other observers have said that zebra finch eggs are light blue or bluish white, but every zebra finch egg I have seen is white.

If you find a nest with more than ten eggs in it or if you note that more than one egg was added to a nest within one day, you are in trouble. The birds are overcrowded and/or there aren't enough nests to go around. You should provide at least two nest sites (boxes, coconuts, baskets, etc.) for each potential pair of birds in a breeding cage or in an aviary.

Although most zebra finch nests are side-opening with dark interiors, you may find some open nests, especially in crowded or warm situations. This is fine so long as the nest building doesn't take precedence over the baby rearing.

In a one-pair cage you control the amount of nesting material. In an aviary you cannot. Birds will steal grass and feathers from each other to build nests—even to build roosting nests—but not if you supply enough nesting material.

If you provide nest bowls, baskets, boxes and coconuts, you will probably discover that the side entrance small enclosure is the favorite site, but when and where you expect it least, a pair will build an open nest and rear a big brood of perfect babies. Don't fight it.

Opposite: *A chestnut-flanked zebra finch. Serious breeders strive for purity of ground color and strength of markings in birds of this particular mutation.*

Left: *A three-day-old zebra finch.*
Below: *A crested male entering a nest with week-old babies. Note that their pinfeathers are beginning to show.*

Above: *The baby zebras in this coconut are about two weeks old.*

INCUBATION

An egg will hatch about twelve to sixteen days after it is laid. Don't wait and worry with a calendar in your hot little hand. The adult birds will leave the nest for hours at a time in warm weather. Incubation will cease when it is really hot. Don't worry; the embryos are tough and their life will continue. Some pairs of adults will sit tighter on their clutches than will other pairs. Don't worry; you don't really even know what to worry about because a tight-sitting bird is not necessarily incubating its eggs. The bird has areas of its body which are devoid of feathers (brood patch) and here the thermal conductivity is good. An insulating layer of feathers between the egg and the brood patch nulls the heat transfer; therefore a tight-sitting bird is no proof of egg incubation. Don't worry; at least 75% of the eggs in your breeding cage or aviary will hatch in spite of everything that you may worry about and those things you may neglect to worry about.

THE WAIF

Sometimes a baby bird will be pushed out of the nest by its siblings or by the accident of clasping its parent when that bird takes wing. On other occasions one or both parents desert the nest or are lost. Well,

regardless of the cause, all is not lost if you have a nest of some other zebras or related species at about the same stage of development.

The options are nearly unlimited. You can swap fledglings which are in trouble with a good chance that their survival rate will improve as a result of your manipulations. If the risk of death is imminent, it is obvious that any action you take is better than no action at all.

Dehydration and cold are the two big problems you must overcome. Imagine that you pick up a pinfeathered zebra finch—say ten days old—from the cage or aviary floor. Its crop is empty and it's cold. You don't know which nest it came from—there are several with same-size fledglings in the area.

First, hold the bird in your cupped hand and blow air from your mouth over it. This air is warm (over 95°F) and it is moist. It contains carbon dioxide (CO_2) which stimulates respiration in animals. Hopefully this treatment will rejuvenate the bird within twenty minutes or less.

Next, get a little sweetened water into its crop. A few drops from a clean insulin syringe will suffice. You may also want to feed the bird if your manual dexterity is good. This can be accomplished by dampening a broomstraw with water and

A pair of zebra finches on a natural wood perch. Tree branches make excellent perches due to the fact that each branch offers a variety of widths. One must be sure, however, that the branches have never been sprayed with poisonous chemicals.

picking up some husked seeds on the end of the straw. These may be rubbed off into the squeaker's mouth as you hold the bird in your hand. If you have trouble getting the seeds husked, try moistened bread.

Remember that tens of thousands of parrots and parrotlike birds have been hand raised—this is nothing new. The only problem is the matter of size. Finches start out very, very small.

After providing warmth and a drink and perhaps a meal, you should choose a nest in which to place the young bird. I don't recommend an incubator and a brooder and a routine of hand-feeding for raising every finch waif. Just get it back on its feet

The birds in these three photos are all normal and healthy. Their crops and bellies are full. They should soon be banded by their owner. Aside from the bands, the parent birds will give them all the care they need.

and then promptly relocate it with others of the same or slightly younger age. This will give the waif an advantage. Don't end up with more than eight babies in a nest—this would overly burden the parents.

A zebra waif may be placed in a nest of society finches with a good chance of success. Society (Bengalese) finches make wonderful foster-parents for all related Australian and Oriental finches—and some African species too!

THE YOUNG

The young could hardly be called "naked" since they are very downy for a week or so. You may even lose sight of them in a feather-lined nest. By the tenth day, the permanent feathers begin to show and the down disappears. By the third day, they cry faintly for food. By the end of a week they make a racket that can be heard one hundred feet away. Both parents feed the young on the same food they have been eating. Offer soaked and sprouted seeds, halfripe grass seeds from a lawn and extra hard-boiled egg. The parents also swallow husked seeds, leaves and insects and regurgitate them into the gullets of the babies. Babies' eyes open on the tenth day plus or minus two days.

A three-week-old bird will leave the nest during the day, but it may return at night. In another six weeks it may lay an egg! Really! Frequently the first clutch by juveniles is abandoned and there is a definite danger of egg-binding when very young females are allowed to breed.

Juveniles have dark brown or blackish bills which gradually become orange or red by the sixth week after hatching. Old birds have redder and more brightly (less brown) colored bills than do young birds.

Under ideal conditions the adults may rear two clutches, one right after the other. When this happens the female will stay with the new eggs and the male will feed the previous nest of birds. Adults in their sixth year will still rear large clutches of healthy, robust young. The human effort involved is really minimal, especially considering the bird's productivity. No wonder zebras are among the least expensive of cage-birds.

Some breeders make a big thing about separating the sexes to limit production to four clutches per year, and they also keep the juveniles apart to prevent breeding by birds younger than eight months. I keep my birds, all of them, in one large aviary. They do their thing on their own schedule and don't seem to suffer a bit.

You should be aware,

In addition to being easy to breed, zebra finches are good singers.

however, that many aviculturists avoid letting their birds breed freely in one large aviary, because under such a system you have much less control over the pairing of birds and therefore over the colors produced. They also feel that it can lead to egg-binding.

FOSTERING

Some species of finches are difficult to propagate. Fertile eggs are laid, but incubation is interrupted or terminated or the fledglings are not fed. Here is where the zebra finch gets into the act.

Zebra finches, and society finches also, are frequently used on a routine basis as foster parents for other seedeating caged finches. Remember that a zebra finch is a seedeater and remember also that its young lower their bodies and twist their necks as they beg for food. By contrast, a young canary will stretch its neck full length as it anticipates a meal. So, match up those species which eat seeds and twist their necks. A zebra simply won't foster a canary.

Gouldian finches have been "factory" bred by withdrawing their eggs for placement under sitting zebras and societies even when the parent Gouldians were perfectly capable of rearing their own young. In this case the procedure is simply a matter of economics for competitive commercial breeders. I don't recommend it; I simply mention it in passing.

To make fostering work, you will need to have a zebra laying at the same time as the problem bird is laying. This isn't as difficult as it might seem. Just keep about three pairs of zebras for each pair of the difficult species and you will never be off more than a few days. Additionally, you can hold most eggs for five or six days at room temperature while you wait for the opportune moment to make the switch.

Don't finger the eggs. Use a small plastic spoon. This will reduce the rejection rate since your own body oils and odor will not enter the baby's system.

Fostering is not an aviary technique, but it should be done with caged pairs for best results. Don't be surprised by all this manipulation—remember that Mother Nature does it all the time with cowbirds and some cuckoo species. Then it is called nest parasitism.

Opposite: *A trio of male zebra finches.*

Nourishment

FOOD

Remember that your birds are locked in your cage with a basic diet of millet, which you bought from a pet dealer who bought it from a distributor who bought it from a wholesale grain merchant who bought it from a farmer who might have neglected to fertilize the millet field where he planted the seed. A wild bird, sensing a lack of an essential nutrient, will search it out. When you keep a captive bird you have voluntarily assumed an obligation to provide that bird with at least its essential requirements for good health.

In addition to dry seed, your birds will also enjoy soaked seed. Use the same millet or canary or finch mixture. Prepare it by putting a half teaspoon of seed per bird in a container of water and letting it soak for 24 or 30 hours. Then drain off the water and deliver the damp seed to your birds. Some fanciers rinse it before serving and some don't.

If you soak the seed four to six days it will become sprouted or germinated seed and this, too, is a great food supplement. Both soaked and sprouted seed are especially good for nestlings and young birds just out of the nest and beginning to feed themselves. A hard dry slippery millet seed is indeed a tough nut for a young bird to crack.

Be careful to distinguish between grain and grain husks. Many a beginning fancier has starved his birds by mistaking empty hulls of grain for whole grain. Some fanciers dump the feed dishes on schedule and start anew with fresh grain daily. Others winnow the grain with a small machine which is available through specialized bird supply houses. Still others winnow the grain by blowing on it, which is a dusty bother and may be dangerous to your health. One neat and economical approach is to dump the uneaten grain and hulls on a damp turkish towel or a dish of damp earth and then the uneaten grain will soak and germinate and sprout while the birds pick it over.

Another food supplement that you can prepare and which is worth trying is adapted from one developed by Hylton Blythe, Thorpe Bay, Essex, England and first published in *Aviculture Magazine* in 1957:

— 1 lb. bread rusk (this is a bread which has been sliced and then baked crisp in an oven at relatively low heat)
— 2 oz. powdered dry skim milk
— 1 oz. wheat germ
— 1 oz. bran
— 1 oz. peanut oil
— 1 oz. cod-liver oil

Mix the two oils and combine with the crushed rusk. Then add

The zebra finch is not a difficult bird to feed; it does, however, require a nutritious balanced diet in order to reach its breeding potential.

the other ingredients, mix and store in a tin or refrigerate until required. Then, moisten with water and feed only what the birds will clean up in a few hours. This formula is obviously higher in fat, protein and vitamins A, B and D than a diet of millet and canary seed. Herein lies its benefit to your birds.

Do you know how to make French toast? Most recipes contain milk and beaten eggs soaked into bread which is then fried in butter or margarine on a griddle. Here is a high-protein, high-fat, high-vitamin food supplement. Your birds will eat it as avidly and as frequently as you do. Do you usually put just a little honey on it? That's how zebra finches like it. Just bear in mind, as always, that millet is the basic food.

I fed an aviary with about 25 pairs of zebras and their young on a basic diet of millet (the color was immaterial) and water. They consumed about ¾ of a cupful daily. The supplements from time to time were canary seed, fresh sliced wheat bread, lettuce, spinach, garden grass, diced hard-boiled chicken eggs, boiled eggshells, cuttlebone and sea salt. I know they love spray millet, but for 50 or 60 birds this must be only an occasional expensive treat. They may also have consumed some webworms (larvae of web moths), web moths, mealworms and other insects; I have no way of positively knowing.

The food you provide should be fresh and clean. There should be no odor of spoilage and no mold. Water should be provided fresh daily in a clean container. You should assume that all your birds are diseased and parasitized even when they are in perfect health and treat them accordingly. Since infection often takes the path of food and water, your primary responsibility is to serve up these things in absolutely clean utensils. This really isn't difficult. You might find that the easiest way is to have two grain dishes and two watering trays. Use each pair on alternate days and scour them on the off day. This might take you all of two minutes of additional time.

I simply take it for granted that my birds will defecate in their food tray and bathe in their drinking water. They have never disappointed me on either item.

If you keep your birds caged you will probably get more production and you will certainly have better control over pair selection, but you will spend more time cleaning and filling the water and feed dispensers. Both systems work. You take your choice.

Incidentally, the floor of the indoor part of my aviary is

Zebra finches love to be together. One must take care, however, not to crowd too many birds into too small an area.

covered with about two inches of dry seed hulls and bird droppings. It is soft, dry and odorless. There is no dust problem. The hulls have accumulated over the course of about two years. I consider this an important technique. There are some webworms, mealworms and dermestid (scavenger) beetles in this floor litter. Great! The webworms and mealworms consume uneaten grain and then the birds eat the worms. The few birds that do die are consumed quickly by the dermestid beetles.

WATER

Chlorine is frequently added to municipal water supplies to reduce odors and reduce the possibility of transmission of diseases. Some birds tolerate small amounts and others seem to resent it. Fortunately, chlorine escapes into the air if water is left standing with a large surface exposed. Agitation helps. Boiling helps, but for zebra finches it really is unnecessary.

If your water is heavily chlorinated, simply draw off what you need into gallon plastic milk bottles. Fill each bottle up to the level where the bottle begins to neck down, say three quarts, and let it stand uncorked for a day or

If you keep a number of birds in one aviary, be sure to provide sufficient amounts of food for all the birds in question.

A gray male zebra finch and a fawn male zebra finch. Note the bright cheek patches on both birds.

two. Hot tap water will give up chlorine even faster.

Water temperature is not an issue with this species of finches. Serve it at room temperature; if it is cooler, it will soon warm up to room temperature. The same goes for bath water. These birds love to bathe. Some will do it twice daily if you leave water out for them.

This is where an anodized aluminum rustproof cage earns its keep. Generally the tray on the bottom of the cage gets the punishment from grits, bird droppings and water.

Your birds will drink their bath water and bathe in their drinking water. Don't let it trouble you; surely it doesn't trouble Mother Nature. A depth of ¾ of an inch of water seems ideal for the bath. A young bird might drown in anything deeper. I use a Pyrex pie plate in the aviary. To catch most of the bath splash, the pie plate is set in a large shallow plastic tray. The important thing about the water, whether it's used for drinking or bathing or both, is that it be clean and fresh.

Sunbathing is another form of bathing that zebra finches will indulge in whenever the opportunity affords. They are usually busy doing things throughout the daylight hours, but they are opportunists and when the sun shines, they will spread their feathers and soak in some sun rays. If the sunlight gets to your birds through a glass window, it will have lost that vitally important ingredient, ultraviolet, which is the form of radiant energy that triggers the creation of vitamin D, and without vitamin D they cannot grow strong bones or produce hard-shelled eggs.

If you house your birds in an outdoor aviary, you may discover that they capture ants and rub themselves with them or that they stand over an anthill and permit the ants to crawl over them. The ants are of the non-stinging varieties and the birds known to do this include 200 species in 30 of the 56 passerine families. Whether zebras also

indulge is for you to find out. At this moment, positive evidence is lacking.

If your birds do it, at least we think we know why. It seems that formic acid and other similar chemicals generated by many species of ants will keep lice away. Other liquids produced by ants may aid in feather maintenance. Among the Estrildidae, waxbills are known to "ant" and we know that some waxbills have hybridized with zebra finches, so you can go from there.

Dust bathing is another activity your birds may indulge in if you provide the ingredients. Bone dry fine sand or earth is worked into the plumage and then it is shaken out, perhaps for feather maintenance or perhaps for louse control. Some species bathe first in dust and then in water when the situation permits. The common house sparrow *Passer domesticus* is a good example of a bird which exhibits this behavior.

MOLTING

Your birds will probably molt once a year beginning in July or August and continue for about two months. They will never be unable to fly nor will they ever appear bald or naked. A feather here, a feather there—you won't miss them. You may notice them on the floor or a nestmaker may

A pair of zebra finches in a basket-type nest. Breeding pairs of zebra finches should be given an especially nutritious diet and should be in excellent condition before they are bred.

collect them to line the egg cavity.

Don't fuss with special foods to carry them through the molt—if they are properly nourished they will manage to manufacture a few feathers from what they had been eating all along.

If a feather grows in twisted or broken, you might want to pluck it rather than wait six months or up to a year for the next molt. If you pull a feather, it will be replaced in less than a month.

A baldheaded bird is probably suffering from a lack of vitamins—most likely vitamin C.

HOUSING

This section may cause some acrimonious debate, but I never promised you a rose garden. To begin at the beginning, the zebra finch is a dry land bird. It is not found in damp places such as marshes or rain forests. Of course it needs water for drinking and it likes water for bathing; however, its natural habitat is a dry one.

To keep a cage or an aviary dry, even the spray caused by

Nourishment

bathing birds and the moisture in their droppings should be disposed of promptly. You can accomplish this in cages by using newspaper bottoms and changing them frequently. Aviaries are another matter. You cannot conveniently blanket the floor with newspaper. Waifs will get lost under the edges, vermin will tear it up—it just doesn't work. Something that does make a fine floor cover is the accumulated husks of countless seeds eaten by the birds over the course of years. Yes, years! And all those droppings too! This litter quickly absorbs water and then disperses it for rapid evaporation.

When I started with the birds two years ago, the floor was just

Greens are an important part of the zebra finch diet, but be sure that they are not given too often.

Sufficient protein is necessary for the breeding female, as protein allows the hen to produce healthy eggs.

a bare kitchen-type linoleum. I threw in about ten pounds of dry grass cuttings and for the next two years I let nature take its course. Nothing was removed. The husks of several hundred pounds of seeds, the bodies of a dozen birds that died of old age or accident, the remains of nests with feathers and droppings—all this remains where it fell.

The aviary is dry, clean and odorless. The birds are in absolutely perfect health. They are actively breeding throughout the year. Pigeon keepers have known this for years; they always leave dry droppings on the floor of the loft.

Mealworms consume the uneaten seeds and dermestid beetles eat the bodies of those few fatalities. The birds probably eat a few of the mealworm grubs. Life goes on.

The area of the indoor aviary is about 100 square feet with an average height of five feet. It will support 50 to 75 birds. When the population exceeds 75 I cut back to 50 in one swoop. This way there is less disturbance to nesting pairs. Since I don't select mated pairs for disposal, there are bound to be some losses in the nests.

Now I know that some people, experienced aviculturists among them, are horrified by my system for various reasons, and I also know that it simply won't appeal to or be a practical method for fanciers who don't have the same type of housing setup as I do. Therefore I'm not recommending that my system be used by everyone—I'm just pointing out that I do things this way and have no problem.

Incidentally, a nesting female with two eggs in a half-coconut lost her mate this way, but she continued alone to raise her little family. Worse yet, it was an open nest and was so full of grass that the babies fell out when only about a week old. This points up one added advantage of the soft floor. From time to time you will pick up a waif that fell out of its nest. If there is an inch or two of chaff on the floor, it will cushion the crash and the baby will have a good chance for survival if you warm it in your hand, breathe on it, squirt a few drops of sweetened water down its gullet with a syringe and pop it back into a nest with other babies of about the same size. Which nest? Any nest. These birds are social and nearly any brooding or feeding adult will brood or feed nearly any baby zebra finch or, for that matter, nearly any baby bird with similar habits. Zebras will rear society (Bengalese) finches and the societies will reciprocate.

At the time of this writing there are about 40 zebras in my aviary. Over the past two years I have sold or given away at least 50. All of these came from an initial stock of about a dozen. The nests have been moved, taken apart and shaken repeatedly, but even with all this disturbance, life goes on. The essentials for their survival are really simple but each ingredient is really important. These birds do get:

Rest. Every night they are left strictly alone all night. There is a dim night light which also provides a spot of warmth. No cats or mice annoy them.

Fresh water. Every day the water is changed whether they need it or not.

Fresh food. Every day they get all the fresh bright seeds they can eat.

Variety of food. Daily they get fresh raw leafy vegetables, hard-boiled egg, bread, salt, eggshells, cuttlebone and grits.

Dry warm perches at night. The inside aviary is large enough to provide ample space

An open-air aviary is an excellent housing plan for zebra finches. Be sure, however, that the birds are not overly exposed to drafts. In addition, be sure that there are no poisonous plants in the aviary.

for each bird to perch or to find a nest box for roosting.

Fresh air and sunlight. The outside flight is never closed. The birds are free to go outside anytime. They sun themselves, bathe in the raindrops and even eat snow in wintertime.

The minimum space for one pair of breeders is 15 by 15 by 24 inches long (3½ cubic feet). Cages this approximate size are available through your pet dealer, if he does not already stock them. It doesn't matter if the cage is made of basket type fibers, wood dowels or rustproof wire; regardless, an easily removable bottom tray is desirable for easy and thorough cleaning. The cage you would use for a singing canary or a budgie is simply too small for breeding zebras.

Another approach to caging breeders is to put as many as five or six pairs in a sixteen cubic foot cage. Hang nest baskets in the upper corners and mid-height corners as well. Try to have twice as many nest baskets and/or boxes as pairs of birds in the cage.

Still another approach is the walk-in aviary with nest boxes and baskets hung from the walls and suspended from the ceiling. Of course a large flight is great for the birds. The exercise they get is surely a plus toward their general good health. Your maintenance efforts are also reduced since thirty or even a hundred birds will all eat from one tray, drink from one or two dishes and bathe in one bath tub. The drawbacks are that diseases will be transmitted faster, and breeding birds will find territories harder to establish. This could lead to deserted nests and nests so full of eggs that no one bird could possibly incubate them all.

Regardless of the size of the cage or aviary, the perches should not be covered with sandpaper or other abrasives. Ideally, the diameters of various perches should range from pencil lead to that of your index finger so that the birds will not always flex their toes exactly the same way.

The zebra will adapt itself to a cage only two feet long, and a pair will successfully produce clutch after clutch of their own or foster young. They do better in aviaries if we consider the effort expended by the bird keeper, but for production and control of color, cages 15″ x 15″ x 24″ long for each pair probably are more appropriate.

You should house one pair or at least three pairs together. Two pairs in the same cage will probably fight continuously.

When frightened, your birds will fly toward the light, and if the light happens to be coming through a glass window in an aviary, broken necks and fractured skulls could result. Usually the protection is easy to accomplish. Stretch a cheesecloth-like fabric over the window and fasten it to the frame with thumbtacks or staples. Most of the light will still get in, but collisions will be cushioned.

Another alternative is to paint the window glass inside with a powder type cleanser. These materials, even if applied thinly, will suffice to warn the birds.

A breeding pair of gray zebra finches. The bill of the female bird is usually lighter in color than that of the male.

Genetics

GENETICS IN GENERAL

Gregor Mendel (1822-1884), the abbot of the Augustinian monastery in Brünn, Moravia and father of the study of genetics, was wonderfully smart. He concentrated on just a few clearly defined, easily recognized, pairs of variables. He kept accurate records. He chose an organism (the pea) which was easy and quick to propagate and which produced relatively large numbers of offspring. Here he demonstrated to the world for eternity that he was smart.

He was also very lucky because the plant he chose just naturally had several easily recognized inheritable features which were simply dominant over several other inheritable features which were simply recessive.

Now, simple dominance and simple recessiveness are not typical in nature. Most creatures are not quite totally black or totally white, but rather they exhibit varying shades of gray. I use the word gray loosely. It could be size or shape or color pattern or feather arrangement or blood type. Fortunately for Mendel, the peas he chose provided a perfect model for a simple, basic and relatively easy analysis of inheritance. It was the first step and he performed it masterfully.

But what if? What if Gregor J. Mendel started with the wild gray zebra finch and one or two wild color variations that crop up in Australia from time to time? I predict that he would have fallen flat on his face. In addition to simple dominant and simple recessive traits, the zebra sometimes exhibits incomplete dominance, intermediate characters, sex linkages and other perfectly reasonable but very complicated genetic traits which make a Mendelian chart undecipherable to a layman no matter how well educated the layman may be in other disciplines of study.

So this is the rub. We do have a lot of information about zebra finch color inheritance, but much of it is difficult to chart or to explain with a few ordinary words. Most textbooks in genetics even provide glossaries that run on for several pages! Let's do the best we can with what we've got.

Those of us who read the Bible and also breed livestock must be aware that what Jacob did with Laban's sheep and goats in Genesis 30:32-43 was surely a miracle. He mated Laban's

Opposite: *Zebra finches provide a wide range of color variations for the breeder who enjoys a challenge.*

animals in front of streaked branches and the animals brought forth streaked young.

Since that event, the short-term effect of environment on heredity has been exaggerated time and time again by all sorts of people for all sorts of reasons. Typical was (or is) the attempt by the USSR Communists to foist the theories of Lysenko on the rest of the world. For years there was a propaganda push from Russia to get the world to believe that wheat could, if subjected to environmental pressures, be changed in one generation into a plant with an entirely new natural history.

What Lysenko claimed in his colossal hoax was that he could create new strains of wheat by subjecting the plants to environmental stress. This would have been great not only for their lagging agricultural economy but also for their philosophy.

Yes, Darwin's Galapagos finches did evolve in several directions over eons to specialize in their environmental niches and new species do prove the point but no, zebra finches will not grow feathers on their feet if we blow cold air on them. And even if they did, their offspring would not be feather-footed as a result.

If we want a variant from the normal wild color of the native Australian zebra finch, we must first find a chance mutation, a genetic freak of nature, and then through selective breeding and application of Mendelian Laws we may be able to fix this trait in a true breeding strain. Remember that for 100 plus years, zebra finches have been bred in cages with vertical bars, but we still don't have any vertically striped birds; and we won't until and unless a mutation is born with a gene for this trait.

How then all these color varieties of zebras today? And crested birds too? Simple. Each and every one resulted from a chance mutation which was then propagated by bird breeders who carefully and thoughtfully inbred the offspring until pure strains were established. Several routes, depending on the nature of the genetic trait, were taken. These genetic traits may be considered separately as we get started.

First is simple dominance. Here the genetic trait need come from only one parent in order to be evident in the offspring. The normal gray color of the wild· Australian zebra finch is governed by a dominant genetic factor.

Next, consider the simple recessive trait. Here a plant, fish, bird or whatever would need the same trait from each parent before it would be evident as a color variation from the normal.

A cream male zebra finch. Before trying to breed a cream-colored zebra, determine whether the bird is a dominant cream or a recessive cream.

Next, be aware that some genetic traits are sex-linked recessives. These ride on the same chromosomes which determine the sex of the bird and this complicates the picture because a male needs two such inputs to have the particular color or other trait appear, but a female bird needs only one such gene.

The convention among geneticists who study birds is to assign the symbols $x(z)$ $x(z)$ to a male and $x(z)$ $y(w)$ to a female. Call it an $xy(zw)$ system and forget it throughout the remainder of this book. We can and will operate here at a simpler level and still be accurate.

GENETICS APPLIED TO ZEBRAS

The puzzles of genetics as applied to birds are one of the great challenges to serious bird breeders, but, fortunately, a novice can have a rewarding experience without any damage to his pets. Any healthy mature male zebra finch may be mated with any healthy mature female zebra finch and they will breed avidly and will likely produce more healthy young than the owner can house. Bear in mind that in 1979 the wholesale cash price to distributors dealing with large numbers of common mixed zebras in the U.S. was about one-third of the final retail price; the costs of handling, feeding, unavoidable loss, transportation, etc., all had to be absorbed in the spread between wholesale and retail prices. The unassailable fact is that some breeder was able to sell thousands of zebra finches at considerably less than one-third of the retail price of the birds and still make enough profit to remain in business. This should

It is in the best interests of the zebra finch breeder to obtain the best possible birds from which to breed.

teach you two things. First is that breeding zebra finches for the mass market is highly competitive, and a difference of a few pennies in your cost might drive you into bankruptcy court. The second is that breeding zebra finches is really quite easy.

What is not at all easy is to be able to produce show-quality birds of predictable color. This is where we separate the men from the boys and the sheep from the goats.

If you are interested in color you will have to follow one of two paths. The first path is to study bird genetics in a formal way. A high school or undergraduate college course is only the beginning. From that point you should go to books on avian genetics. After you catch up with all that, you will discover that it will still take a good deal of your time just to keep up with new developments in this field of study.

The second path is empirical. It requires that you obtain data, based on the experiences of breeders, which has accumulated in the literature over the past 100 years. You need not know why something happens but simply what will happen when birds of certain parentage and certain colors are mated. Don't get the idea that the empirical method is easy. The combinations and

A penguin zebra finch.

permutations are tremendous. The genetic information packed in just one chromosome in the nucleus of one ovum or sperm cell will be just as powerful and complicated regardless of whether you approach your bird's breeding efforts by applying genetic theory or empirical knowledge. I suggest you start with some breeding stock of known pedigree and approach your educational process by way of the empirical method. If as time goes on you wish to get involved with the scientific theory, you will find the going easier as a result of the empirical knowledge already acquired. A small sample of the first lesson of the genetic theory applied to zebras appears in this book, primarily to show you what you are missing.

GLOSSARY OF GENETIC TERMS

If you read much bird breeding literature you will see a few words which deserve short, simple explanations. Here is a very brief glossary of genetic terms, some of which apply only to theory and some of which are used by practical, empirical bird breeders. I recommend you breeze through them now and refer back to them later as they appear in other things you may read.

DOMINANT: A genetic trait which requires but one gene of a pair to make itself evident.

HETEROZYGOUS: See Split.

HOMOZYGOUS: Pure for a particular genetic trait. The same gene appears in the same place on a matched pair of chromosomes. May be pure dominant or pure recessive.

HYBRID: Split.

PURE: Homozygous.

RECESSIVE: A genetic trait which does not become evident unless two matched genes are aligned.

SPLIT: Heterozygous; that is, impure (hybrid) for a particular genetic trait. Different genes appear in the same place on a matched pair of chromosomes.

ALBINO: An individual which lacks pigment. If it is a technically genuine 100% true absolute albino it is all white and its eyes are pink. In nature there are very few totally true absolutes.

BASICS

The process of sexual reproduction common to most but not all higher animals hinges on a biological process in which certain cells are formed with only one-half of the genetic material usually found in animal tissue. Such a male cell (sperm) meets such a female cell (ovum) and the resulting fertilization of the ovum by the sperm creates the first cell of a new organism with its full complement of genetic material. Half of it came from the male parent and half from the female. Now, that was easy, wasn't it? (Incidentally, one exception which comes readily to my mind is a race of female lacertilian lizards.)

Sex is determined genetically much as is color or size or form, and we know through experimentation and research that we can assign symbols to these genetic traits and predict, statistically, the appearance of offspring yet unborn by knowledge of the genetic makeup of the parents.

One set of symbols which gets a lot of use is the sex symbols. A male mammal is shown symbolically as *xy* and a female mammal as *xx*. When a male mammal *xy* is mated with a female mammal *xx* we chart the union thusly:

male

x	xx	xx
y	xy	xy
	x	x female

As you can see, over the long haul, the ratio of offspring from a mating of a male and a female is one-to-one, for which we can be grateful. Now, interestingly and confusingly, mammals and birds don't do it quite the same way. The designators for sex in birds are: *xx* for a male and *xy* for a female. The same principles are at work, but the bird with the two matching genes (xx) is a male and the mismatch (xy) is the female.

Now, sex-linked color in birds doesn't ride on a *y,* but it may sometimes ride on an *x.* This means that a color trait which

A marked white male zebra finch.

happens to be sex-linked recessive and appears on only one *x* gene could be masked by a complementary dominant *x* gene in a male. If, perchance, it appears in a female, this recessive color will be apparent to you since no dominant color gene rides on the *y* to mask this recessive trait. To bring out the same recessive color in a male requires that both *x* genes carry that inheritable color factor. The chestnut-flanked white and the fawn are sex-linked in zebras. The so-called albino or pseudo-albino is sometimes sex-linked recessive and sometimes a simple recessive. More about this later.

COLOR

The easiest way to understand zebra finch color is to commence with the show standards and color standards of the British Zebra Finch Society as published in their handbook and reprinted here by their kind permission.

Normal cock. Eyes dark. Beak red. Feet and legs red. Head and neck dark grey, wings grey. Breast bar jet black. Throat and upper breast zebra striped, grey with darker lines running from cheek to cheek continuing down to chest bar. Underparts white, may have some fawnish shading near vent and thighs. Cheek lobes dark orange. Tear markings black and distinct. Tail black with white bars, side flankings reddish brown with clear white spots. **Hen.** As for cock minus chest barring, lobe and flank markings. Beak paler in color. Tear markings black and distinct. A lighter shade of normal is recognised. Show faults: Brown shading on wings and mantle.

White, Cock and Hen. Eyes dark. Beak red. Feet and legs pink. Pure white all over. Hens usually have beaks of a paler shade of red. Show faults: Colored spangles on mantle.

Fawn Cock. Eyes dark. Beak red. Feet and legs pink. Head, neck and wings deep even fawn. Breast bar dark. Throat and upper breast light fawn with zebra lines running from cheek to cheek continuing down to breast bar. Underparts white, may have some fawnish shading near vent and thighs, cheek lobes dark orange, tear markings same shade as breast bar. Tail dark barred with white. Side flankings reddish brown with even clear white spots. **Hen.** As other hens but of the same shade of fawn as cocks. Show faults: Variation in color between cock and hen of pairs.

Dominant Cream (Dilute Fawn) Cock. Eyes dark. Beak red. Feet and legs pink. Again all shades from deep cream to pale cream. Markings in cocks to be in general tone to match depth of diluteness. Tear markings same shade as breast bar. Tail deep cream with white bars. **Hen.** As other hens but of the same

Opposite: *A fawn yellow-beaked zebra finch. Note the rich yellow color of the beak.*

A male penguin zebra finch. The distinctive lacing pattern does not show until the second full molt.

shade to match the cocks. Show faults: Variation in color between cock and hen of pairs and variation in color of individual birds. Fawn shadings. Indistinct markings on cocks.

Pied Cock and Hen. Eyes dark. Beak red, feet and legs pink. Any other colors broken with white approximately 50% of each color (white underparts not to be included in this 50%). Cock to retain cock markings in broken form on cheeks, flanks and chest. Tear markings distinct but can be broken. Show faults: Loss of cock markings which should be shown in broken form. Exhibition pairs to be matched for pied markings.

Chestnut-Flanked White Cock. Eyes dark, beak red. Feet and legs pink. Head, neck, back, and wings as white as possible. Underparts pure white. Breast bar as near black as possible. Tear markings same shade as breast bar. Cheek lobes orange. Tail white with bars. Color to match chest bar. Flank markings reddish brown with clear white spots. **Hen.** As other hens to match cocks. May have light head markings. Show faults: Markings too pale in the cock.

Penguin (Normal) Cock. Eyes dark. Beak red. Feet and legs pink. Head, neck and wings a light even silver grey, with flights, secondaries and coverts edged with a paler shade of grey giving a laced effect. (This lacing does not show to full advantage until the second full molt.) Underparts from beak to vent pure white without any trace of barring. Cheek lobes pale orange to pale cream to match body color of bird. Tail silvery grey barred with white. Side flankings reddish brown with clear white spots. **Hen.** As other hens but with cheek lobes white. (There can be Penguin forms of the other colors.) Show faults: Barring on chest.

Recessive Silver (Dilute Normal) Cock. Eyes dark. Beak red. Feet and legs pink. Head, neck and mantle medium bluish grey, wings grey. Throat and upper breast zebra striped, bluish grey with darker lines running from cheek to cheek

Artist's rendering of a cream male zebra finch (top) and a silver female zebra finch (bottom).

Male normal penguin zebra finch (top), male fawn zebra finch (center), and recessive silver female zebra finch (bottom).

continuing down to chest bar. Chest bar dark grey. Tear marks distinct and to match color of chest bar. Cheek lobes medium orange. Underparts white, sometimes slightly shaded near thighs and vent. Flankings light reddish brown with clear white spots. Tail dark with white bars. Cock markings should be clear and distinct with only slight dilution. **Hen.** As other hens but of the same shade to match the cocks. Show faults: Variation in color between cock and hen of pairs and variation in color of individual birds. Fawn shadings. Indistinct markings on cock. Color too dark or too light.

Recessive Cream (Dilute Fawn) Cock. Eyes dark. Beak red. Feet and legs pink. Head, neck and mantle medium cream, wings cream. Throat and upper breast zebra striped, cream with darker lines running from cheek to cheek continuing down to chest bar. Cheek lobes medium orange. Underparts white, sometimes slightly shaded near thighs and vent. Flankings light reddish brown with clear white spots. Tail dark cream with white bars. Cock markings should be clear and distinct with only slight dilution. **Hen.** As other hens but of the same shade to match the cocks. Show faults: Variation in color between cock and hen of pairs and variation in color of individual birds. Fawn shadings.

Indistinct markings on cocks. Colors too dark or too light.

Yellow-Beaked Varieties. General coloring as Normal Grey and all other mutations except the beak which should be shades of yellow with the cock birds showing the richest color. There can be a yellow-beaked form of all existing mutations and their composite forms. Yellowbeaks must be exhibited in true pairs of the same mutation. Show faults: As with the normal red-beaked kinds.

A.O.C. In the interest of breeders and exhibitors no new color will be recognized until thoroughly investigated by the Committee. Panel judges are reminded that the Show and Colour Standards must be observed. Zebra Finches can only be shown in true pairs, i.e. a cock and a hen at Patronage Shows. A pair must always consist of two birds of the same mutation.

Now, let's consider these recognized colors and take note of their genetic makeup.

Normal is the color of at least one race of wild Australian zebra finches. It is dominant over most other colors. The exceptions are two dilute mutations known as dominant dilutes. These are silver and cream. The crested feather arrangement is also an independent dominant trait.

In each of these instances a bird with a single gene of that trait will exhibit the trait. These dominants are not sex linked. For example, a normal *dd* when mated to a pure (homozygous) dominant dilute bird *DD* will produce:

(normal)

d	Dd	Dd
d	Dd	Dd
	D	D (dominant dilute)

100% dilute birds, all of which are heterozygous (split) *Dd* for normal. If two pure dominant dilutes *DD* are mated, the offspring will surely be 100% pure dominant dilute.

If two split dominant dilutes (Dd x Dd) are mated, the offspring will be:

D	DD	Dd
d	Dd	dd
	D	d

25% will be pure dominant dilute, *DD*.

50% will be dominant dilute in appearance but will be genetically only half pure-split, heterozygous *Dd*.

25% will be normally colored *dd*. They will have no dominant dilute genetic material to pass on to their descendants.

An Easy Beginning With Normals (NN or Nn) and Albinos (nn)

A) Two homozygous pure dominant *NN* wild color birds are mated. Their offspring (barring a very slim unlikely chance of a new mutation) will resemble the parents.

(normal)

N	NN	NN
N	NN	NN
	N	N (normal)

B) Two homozygous pure recessive *nn* albino birds are mated. Their offspring (again barring a very slim unlikely chance of a new mutation) will resemble both parents. They will be albinos.

(albino)

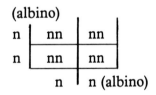

n	nn	nn
n	nn	nn
	n	n (albino)

C) One bird from example A when mated to a bird from example B will produce offspring which all look like A, but every one will be heterozygous (split) for albino.

Opposite: *A lovely penguin zebra finch. Note the laced effect on the wing.*

Opposite top: *A pair of healthy wild type gray zebra finches.* **Opposite bottom:** *The bird that is squatting in this photo may be tired or frightened, but it may be sick. Squatting is not a normal position for a healthy zebra finch.* **Above:** *The cheek patch on this zebra finch shows that it is a male bird.*

Normal x Albino = Normal/Albino. We abbreviate this to read: NN x nn = Nn, and we display it in a more useful form:

(normal)

	Nn	Nn
N	Nn	Nn
N	Nn	Nn
	n	n (albino)

By the empirical method this Nn bird which is heterozygous (split) for albino would be designated:

Normal/Albino or Normal split for albino.

There have been many authors and many authorities since Mendel who have developed their own shorthand and today there are several ways to present the same facts. Here you will find several of the words in common use today in each example to help you as you read about zebras from various sources. The facts are the same, but the words change.

D) A heterozygous (split) hybrid Nn is mated to a normal (pure) NN.

(split)

	NN	NN
N	NN	NN
n	Nn	Nn
	N	N (normal pure)

50% of a large population would be pure (dominant) normal, homozygous, wild type NN.

50% would be split-heterozygous and would look like the normals but would have a recessive gene for albino Nn. Looking at these birds, the parents and their offspring, will resolve nothing. They will all look alike.

E) Two split (heterozygous) Normal/Albino hybrids Nn are mated.

(split)

	NN	Nn
N	NN	Nn
n	Nn	nn
	N	n (split)

25% of the offspring of a large population will be pure (dominant) wild color, homozygous, normal NN.

25% will be albino nn.

50% will be wild color, heterozygous (split) Nn. They will look like NN above, but they will carry the recessive genetic albino trait.

Unfortunately for people who want simple pat answers, this is not the whole story. As you get deeper into the zebra hobby, you will find references to albinism on other loci; that is, located where the genes don't necessarily align. Also there is the matter of leucism. Also there is the matter of sex linkage and also incomplete dominance. Be humble.

When many birds are kept together in an aviary, they may breed indiscriminantly. The birdkeeper should try to pair birds of compatible type and color.

Above: *This fawn penguin (or brown-wing) is surely a female bird. Note the pale beak and the absence of cheek or flank markings.* **Opposite top:** *The fawn zebra finch mutation is sometimes called the Isabelle mutation.* **Opposite bottom:** *A fawn male zebra finch. Lighting sometimes makes birds of one mutation appear to be birds of a different color mutation.*

As you were just previously warned, the genetic factor for the absence of pigment or albinism may be located in any one of several places on the chromosomes in the nucleus of the cell. If two birds, each with one or even two recessive albino genes, are mated and these gene locations do not match up, there will be no albino offspring, regardless of how many young are reared. So two albinos do not necessarily an albino make. What would Mendel have done had he started his genetic investigations with zebra finches? I think he would have quit.

To make matters even more confusing, the albino genetic trait is sometimes linked to sex chromosomes. Now, a male bird has two x chromosomes. This is what makes him a male, xx. On the other hand, the female is that way because she has one x and one y chromosome. We designate a female bird xy. In mammals, it is the other way around.

When albinism or some lesser degree of pigment dilution is linked to sex it rides on the x chromosome only. Let's call the gene for albino c and the gene for non-albino (normal) C. When c and C are both present, the C is dominant and albinism is not apparent. A sex-linked female xy albino would be $x^c y$. A sex-linked male xx, if he were albino, would be $x^c x^c$. Since no color rides on the y chromosomes, the female needs but one albinism gene on her one-and-only x chromosome to make her pink-eyed and all white. Other hereditary factors will also ride on those x chromosomes, but we must ignore them at this time or drown in the morass of our vast pool of knowledge.

Now, I repeat, a female with the designation $x^c y$ would be albino because the y chromosome doesn't carry either c or C gene.

So let's see what happens when a male which is heterozygous for sex-linked albino is mated to such a female:

male		
x^C	$x^C x^c$	$x^C y$
x^c	$x^c x^c$	$x^c y$
female	x^c	y

25% will be $x^c x^c$ colored males
25% will be $x^C y$ colored females
25% will be $x^c x^c$ albino males
25% will be $x^c y$ albino females
That was easy, but don't get puffed up. I omitted partial

Opposite: *A lovely fawn zebra finch. Note the zebra markings on the breast.*

Above: *Zebras picking over a piece of garden grass sod. This is a good practice since the birds are receiving grits and some important trace elements.* **Opposite top:** *A young and healthy zebra finch. Note how the crop bulges.* **Opposite bottom:** *These birds are about three days apart in age. The smaller bird will not catch up in size until the larger bird leaves the nest.*

albinism, also called leucism, and I also omitted those leucinos which appear when certain but not all the pigments are genetically lost.

Dr. Paul A. Buckley, while at the Department of Biology at Hofstra University, pointed out that leucism, unlike albinism, is often dominant—yes, dominant—to normal or wild-type coloration. He goes on to tell us that since the genes which control color are not located in complementary places on the chromosomes, an animal might be leucistic over certain parts of its body and normally colored elsewhere.

Readers may wonder how it can be that all birds are not white if leucism is frequently a dominant trait. One explanation is that in the wild, a leucistic bird stands out like a sore thumb and will be the object of every predator. One hypothesis is that these birds are sexually less

Two white male zebra finches. A good white zebra finch specimen should have no colored markings in its plumage.

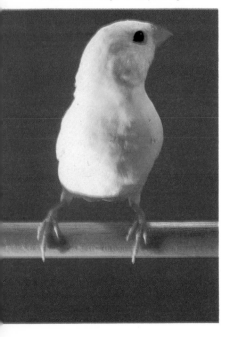

attractive and so are less likely to reproduce themselves. Still another good guess is that with leucism there is often poor vision or less stamina and so the survival of the most fit tends to weed these oddballs out of wild populations. In the cage and aviary, man plays God.

SEX-LINKED GENETIC TRAITS

Sex-linked colors are fawn, chestnut-flanked whites and certain but not all albinos. These characters are not only sex-linked but also are recessive to the normal wild color. The diagrams should help.
Remember:
— xx is a male bird.
— xy is a female bird.
— N is normal wild dominant color.
— n is any sex-linked recessive trait (such as albino or fawn or chestnut-flanked white).
— N and n ride only on x chromosomes. The y chromosome is not a carrier of color genes.

Bear in mind that other genes on other chromosomes may also influence color, but if we don't take these items methodically and one at a time, we will never unravel the mystery.

1) Mate a cock $x^n x^n$ with sex-linked color to a similar looking hen $x^n y$.

The offspring will be colored like their parents and will be genetically identical for these

A marked white female zebra finch.

traits.

2) Mate a normal, homozygous, pure, wild color, $x^N x^N$ cock to a sex-linked albino or fawn or chestnut-flanked $x^n y$ hen.

50% of the offspring will be cocks with normal wild color, but they will be split heterozygous for the sex-linked recessive color.

50% of the offspring will be females and all of them will be normal colored and will have no hidden (split) heterozygous

The four species shown here have all been hybridized with zebra finches. **Left:** *Parrot finch.* **Below:** *Bengalese (society) finch.* **Opposite top:** *Quail finch.* **Opposite bottom:** *Three-colored mannikin.*

genetic trait for sex-linked color.

3) Mate a split cock $x^N x^n$ and a normal gray hen $x^N y$. Both parents are gray of course, but there is that sex-linked recessive gene in the male.

	x^N	y
x^N	$x^N x^N$	$x^N y$
x^n	$x^N x^n$	$x^n y$

25% will be gray females $x^N y$.

25% will be sex-linked colored females (white or fawn or the chestnut-flanked strain) $x^n y$.

4) Mate a wild-colored heterozygous split cock $x^N x^n$ with a sex-linked female $x^n y$ of the same strain.

	x^n	y
x^N	$x^N x^n$	$x^N y$
x^n	$x^n x^n$	$x^n y$

25% of the offspring will be $x^N x^n$ males split (heterozygous) for the sex-linked color. They will be wild colored.

25% of the offspring will be $x^n x^n$ males, pure, sex-linked, recessive, homozygous.

25% will be females $x^N y$ wild color.

25% will be females $x^n y$ displaying the sex-linked color.

The sex-linked albinos mentioned previously are an example of this situation.

Remember that the sex-linked characteristics are independent of each other and also of other genetic traits which may be carried on other chromosomes. If you should mate a chestnut-flanked white male with a sex-linked fawn female the offspring will not simply combine the features of their parents. For an example, let's chart this above-mentioned situation. Call *nc* the gene for white chestnut-flanked and *nf* the gene for sex-linked fawn color.

$x^{nc} x^{nx}$ is the male
$x^{nf} y$ is the female

	x^{nf}	y
x^{nc}	$x^{nc} x^{nf}$	$x^{nc} y$
x^{nc}	$x^{nc} x^{nf}$	$x^{nc} y$

50% of the offspring will be males. They will be designated $x^{nc} x^{nf}$ and they will be neither fawn nor chestnut-sided white, but they will have the normal wild color or some other non-sex-linked color since a sex-linked color characteristic on a male takes two matched genes to produce that color.

50% of the offspring will be females $x^{nc} y$ and all of them will be of the chestnut-flanked white strain.

Further, a dilute silver or cream is also known to be an incompletely dominant trait. One silver bird among the parents will assure silver-colored offspring.

Artist's rendering of a pair of dilute silver zebra finches.

Here it seems that genes located elsewhere—on other chromosomes perhaps—will also exert their influence. This muddies the waters. No one said it was easy.

Now that you have grasped the principle of genetics as applied to zebra finches (and you are thoroughly hooked) this is the appropriate place to mention that a true albino lacks *all* pigment. The feathers must be absolutely white and the eyes pink. If the eyes are brown or even ruby there is some pigment present, and the bird is not a true albino.

Dr. Matthew M. Vriends in his *Handbook of Zebra Finches* points out that to date no pink-eyed zebra finches are known. So, strictly speaking, he calls white zebras pseudoalbino and he is absolutely right.

But this is my book and I take another view. In nature I see few absolutes. Most rules are literally and figuratively shades-of-gray. So let it be with albinos.

Above: *Hardboiled egg is an excellent food supplement, especially for breeding pairs and young birds. Feed the shell along with the yolk and the white.* **Right:** *A pair of long-tailed grassfinches, members of one of the species that has been hybridized with the zebra finch.*

Interbreeding

and Interfering

BREEDING STOCK

You may want to control your breeding operation by caging individual pairs or small groups of pairs. You may keep an aviary with just one color variety and cull out all those that don't match. You may opt for letting nature take its course and provide no control whatsoever over an aviary full of birds. The choice is up to you. The more you control, the better you can predict the outcome, but you must work much harder—more cages to clean, babies to band, records to keep.

My only advice is to start with robust birds and act promptly and ruthlessly to keep the quality up. Inbreeding of defective birds is a game for fools.

As to the breeding stock you start with, be selective. Don't fall in love with the first one-eyed, half-feathered wry-tailed bird you

A lovely gray zebra finch. Some breeders believe that the gray zebra finch is the most reliable breeder.

see. Shop around, pay a fair price and then breed up, not down.

Any zebra finch will mate with any other zebra finch of the opposite sex. Since even white or silver birds can be sexed by study of their bill color and behavior, you should have no trouble on that score.

Any zebra finch old enough to show its colors is old enough to reproduce itself, but many experienced breeders of show quality birds will not permit

breeding with any birds younger than eight months.

Any zebra finch may desert its first nest and then go on to be an excellent producer for the next few years.

Any color variety of zebra finch is capable of raising its own young, but some breeders believe that the wild gray variety is the most reliable producer.

Any age zebra finch may be mated to another. They need not be matched for age.

CROSSBREEDING

Zebras get along well with other bird species. So well, in fact, that there are on record about two dozen crosses between zebras and other species which are known to have produced living young. Some crosses produce the same type of offspring using either sex from either species, and in other cases the sex of each species determines the outcome. Two examples of this outside of aviculture are the horse with the ass or the zebra and the lion with the tiger. In the case of the horse, a stallion mated to a female ass produces a hybrid called a hinny, but a jackass mated to a mare produces a hybrid called a mule. Now, a mule and a hinny do not resemble each other even though the same two species were involved in producing these

Zebra finches need exercise to remain healthy. For this reason, it is imperative that one does not crowd too many birds into a cage or aviary.

hybrid animals. The hinny, incidentally, has a disproportionately larger body compared to its legs, a more bushy tail and a more tractable disposition than does the more common and better known mule.

In the case of the aforementioned lion, it has been hybridized with the tiger and the offspring are called either tigons or ligers, depending on the sexes of the parent species. A tigon does not resemble a liger any more than a hinny resembles a mule, and all of this is analogous to some situations which may result when birds of various species are interbred.

To discuss the product of crossbreeding between the horse and the zebra in this book will surely lead to misunderstandings. Browsers, speed readers and readers from the back to front would never get through the chapter if this aspect were to be explored. Suffice it to say here that there are no records of horses crossbred with birds.

In the cage or the aviary you

The species shown here have been successfully hybridized with the zebra finch. **Opposite top:** Long-tailed grassfinch. **Opposite bottom:** Red-billed fire finch. **Right:** Bicheno's finch. **Below:** Java sparrow.

will find zebra finches able to get on well with many other species. Mixed collections of zebras with virtually all species of exotic finches are common and successful. Zebras in an aviary will mate only with each other and no hybrids will result. To achieve hybrid crosses, selected birds must be paired and isolated, preferably out of the sight and hearing of all other birds.

HYBRIDS

According to Annie P. Gray in *Bird Hybrids*, Commonwealth Agricultural Bureaux, 1958 (pages 239 and 240), the following zebra hybrids have been reported (unless stated otherwise, the zebra was the male):

— *Chloris chloris*, green finch
— *Erythrura trichroa*, three-colored parrot finch
— *Estrilda atricollis*, quail finch
— *Lagonostica senegala*, red-billed fire finch
— *Lonchura castaneothorax*, chestnut-breasted finch
— *Lonchura domestica*, Bengalese (or society) finch
— *Lonchura malabarica cantans*, African silverbill
— *Lonchura malacca*, chestnut (or three-colored) mannikin
— *Lonchura striata acuticauda*, sharp-tailed finch
— *Padda oryzivora*, Java sparrow

— *Poephila acuticauda*, long-tailed grassfinch
— *Poephila bichenovii*, Bicheno's finch
— *Poephila cincta*, banded grassfinch, parson finch; cross works with either sex (both directions)
— *Poephila modesta*, cherry finch or plum-headed finch; cross works in both directions
— *Poephila ruficauda*, star finch; probably works in both directions
— *Zonaeginthus guttatus*, diamond sparrow; cross works in both directions.

HUMAN INTERFERENCE

Consider the extreme situations; these should provide a frame of reference. In wild Australia, thousands of generations of zebra finches reproduced themselves with no sight or smell or noise or touch of man, but I remember reading an account by a field ornithologist about wild zebras which were captured and caged and bred in the back of a Land Rover while the field investigations continued. This is truly an extreme situation, but it shows how flexible these birds will be if their diet and certain environmental conditions are right.

Your caged birds should be checked daily or not at all when they are nesting. If you plan to

A wild female zebra finch. Zebra finches are adaptable, tolerant birds that make the challenge of breeding accessible to the beginner and challenging to the experienced.

use seamless bands on the babies, the banding should not be your only visit; it may lead to desertion of the nest. If, however, you look into every nest every day, your presence and smell will be part of their environment, and the risk of nest desertion will be minimized. Be reconciled—you will lose one now and then. This happens with humans too. Young zebras frequently desert their first nest and then go on to years and years of successful production.

Your interference should be constructive:

—provide each pair of birds with at least two nest boxes or baskets.

— provide plenty of nesting material, dry grass stems, soft grass clippings and feathers or cotton or wool scraps.

These three species have been crossbred with zebra finches. **Left:** Plum-headed finch. **Below:** Diamond sparrow. **Opposite:** Star finch.

— provide plenty of clean water for bathing; most birds must keep their eggs damp to assure easy pipping at hatching time.

— provide ample fresh food, green vegetables, hard-boiled eggs, cuttlebone, mineral supplements, sprouted seeds and dry seeds; offer the supplements, but never neglect the basic diet ingredient, millet.

— provide quarters that are vermin-free.

— provide a night light.

— provide peace and quiet every night, all night.

BANDS

If you are serious about breeding more than one pair, you should keep track of your birds with bands. There are two basic types of bands. First are the permanent bands which are seamless rings—usually of aluminum and anodized in many permanent colors which you can obtain custom-made with your initials and some system of numbering embossed on the metal. This seamless band remains on the bird for its lifetime. You will slip it on a fledgling when it is about four days old by sliding it over the three forward toes and then past the pad of the foot and up the shank of the lower leg until it clears the rear toenail. If it doesn't get by that rear toenail you can use a toothpick to pull the toe through. The ring then slips down on the lower leg and remains loosely but permanently attached for the life of the bird. Breeders will order bands in a different color every year so that the age will be apparent even without close examination. The Zebra Finch Society chooses a color for each year to help standardize the problem of quick age determination. Of course the number of the band should be recorded in a ledger along with others of that clutch and the numbers of the parent birds.

The second style of band has some sort of seam somewhere. It is a flat plastic springy coil which usually bears a number or a letter. Of course these, too, are available in various colors. Seam bands are usually used by breeders just to keep track of pairs or sexes—combinations of colors on left or right or both feet will provide the information at a glance. Of course they may be removed at the end of a breeding season. Band manufacturers also provide a plierslike tool for applying and removing these springy plastic devices.

Another type of coil band made of plastic is simply a colored spring coil which bears no number. This, too, is useful in an aviary where many pairs might otherwise not be sortable.

Index

94

95

Breeding Zebra Finches
KW-056